Write

your

Kindle Book

with

Free Software

by

Joel Dare

Table of Contents

Introduction

This is a short book. It's short for a couple reasons. First, because you'll find that writing a Kindle book is actually pretty easy when someone explains the basics and walks you through it. You'll probably have a couple challenges the first time, but re-read the instructions and follow them again and it will become easier over time. Second, It's short because I like reading short books and I hope that you will too. Like you, I'm busy doing things I love. I work full time and have dozens of hobbies that keep me busy. I hope you'll be glad this book gets to the point quickly and gives you just the skills you need to get the job done.

Get LibreOffice

First, you'll need the free LibreOffice suite. It includes a word processor, similar to Microsoft Word, that you'll use to write your book. Point your web browser to the URL below and click the big *Download LibreOffice* button on that page.

http://www.libreoffice.org

Once it's downloaded, double-click the icon to install it. Typically you can just accept the defaults for the install. They already have some good documentation on how to install LibreOffice, so I won't walk you through that here. If you need help, the LibreOffice web page has good step-by-step instructions. Those are currently listed under *Get Help* and then *Installation* in the menu at the top of that web page.

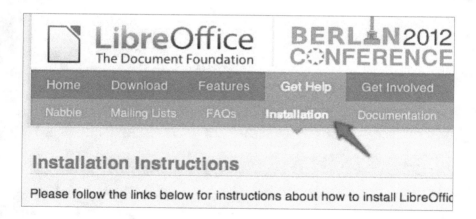

LibreOffice is available for Windows, Mac, and even Linux. The screenshots in this book were taken on a Mac but the program is nearly identical on the other platforms.

Set Page Settings

If you haven't already, go ahead and open LibreOffice. On the first page, select **Text Document** as the type of document to open.

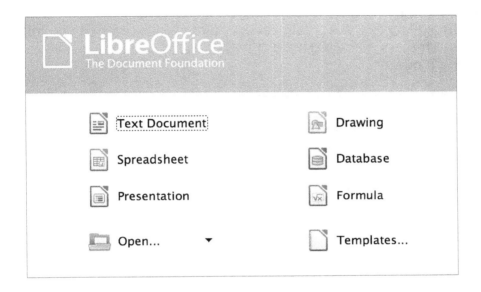

The first thing I like to do is change the document size a bit. This gives you a better feel for how your book will look on the typical Kindle device.

Pull down the **Format** menu and choose **Page**.

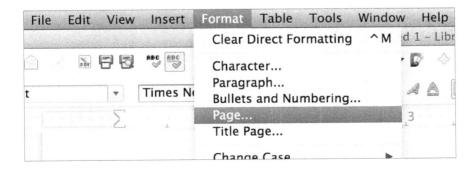

Set the *Width* to 5.5" and the *Height* to 8.5". This is the size of a sheet of letter size paper cut in half. I like this size because it's somewhat universal. It's similar to the aspect ratio on some Kindle devices and it makes a good size for print at home too. If you're outside the United States, you might want to use half of an A4 sheet instead. That would be 148.5mm wide by 210mm high. Either size is fine for this tutorial, we won't talk about dimensions in inches or millimeters much, so it won't matter which option you choose right now.

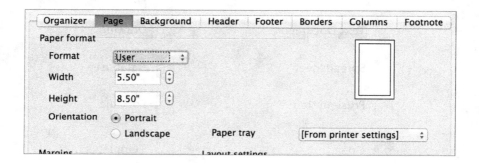

Save As Word Document

Now we need to save the document in *Microsoft Word 97* format.

Select *File*, *Save As* from the menu.

Select *Microsoft Word 97* in the *File type* drop down and click the *Save* button.

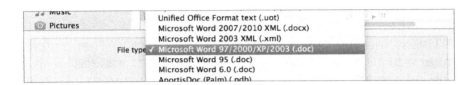

When you're prompted, click the *Use Microsoft Word 97* button to confirm your choice. LibreOffice will ask this question a lot. If you'd like to avoid seeing this dialog over and over again, go ahead and uncheck the box next to *Ask when not saving in ODF format* so that LibreOffice will stop bugging you about it.

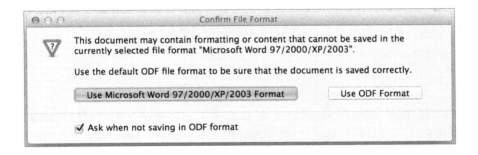

Set Default Paragraph Settings

We need to setup our default paragraph settings so that everything looks as close as possible to the way it will come out on the Kindle device.

From the menu, select *Format*, *Styles and Formatting* to turn on the style dialog. Right click on *Text body*, and then select *Modify*. On the *Indents & Spacing* tab, set the *First line* setting under *Indent* to 0.15" and the *Below paragraph* setting under *Spacing* to 0.15".

This is the first time I mentioned "right click". That simply means to use the mouse button on the right instead of the one on the left (which is the one you typically use). One a Mac it's a two finder tap, but I'll refer to it as a "right click".

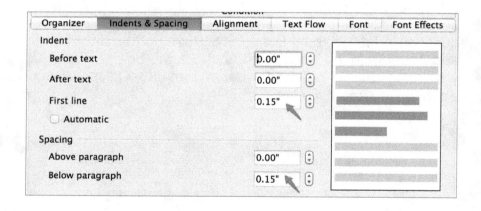

Go to the *Alignment* tab and set *Justified* under *Options*. This is actually optional, but most Kindle devices display their text fully justified, so we might as well look at our text that way as we write.

Creating the Title Page

You've got your document sized and you're on the first page. It must be time for a title. Go ahead and type the name of your title. If you don't know the final name yet, use a temporary name.

We're going to use really large letters on this first page, so keep your title to two or three words per line. Here's what the title of this book looked like on that first page.

Next, lets center the title. Highlight the title and click the center icon in the menu at the top of the page.

Now lets increase the font size a fair amount. I like my title to be twice the size of the rest of my text. Notice that the font size, again in the toolbar at the top of the page, is currently 12. Highlight the title again and use the pulldown to switch it to 24 point.

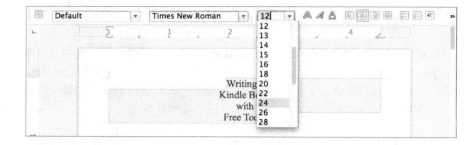

Your title page should now look something like this.

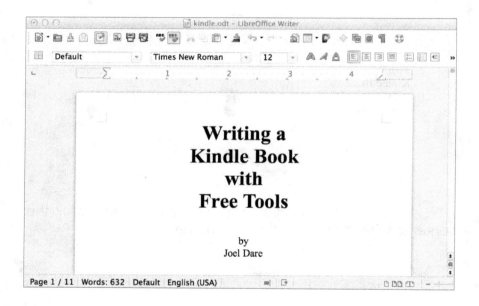

The title will be the only thing on this first page, so now you need to insert a page break after the title to move your cursor to the next page. Use the menu to select *Insert*, *Manual Break*, choose *Page Break* and then hit *OK*.

Your First Section

We're going to create an Introduction page next. This will be the first section in our book. Start by typing the title of the section, "Introduction" then press enter to move to a new paragraph. Enter a bit of introduction text. Your Introduction page should look something like the following image.

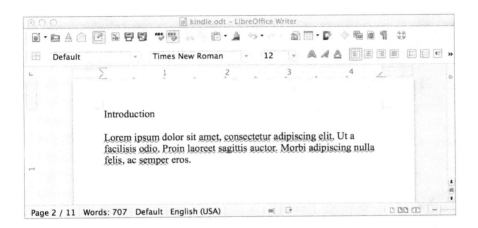

If your page doesn't look like that one, make sure that the formatting is correct. Open the **Format**, **Styles and Formatting** dialog again. Highlight the first paragraph in your introduction, and double click on **Default** in the dialog. This switches the highlighted text to the default format. Any time text in your document looks odd, highlight it and switch it to that default format. That will typically fix it.

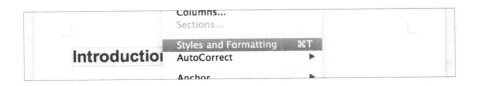

Now we need to set the word *Introduction* to be a heading. This will both increase it's font size and add it to the table of contents. We'll talk about the table of contents more later.

For now, highlight the word *Introduction* and double click on **Heading 1** in the *Styles and Formatting* dialog. If it's not open, select **Format**, **Styles and Formatting** from the menu.

You should notice that it's font size and weight changes.

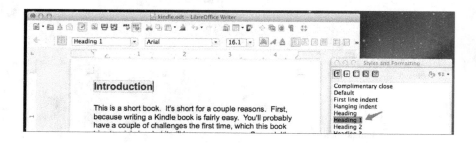

Your introduction is now finished and should look something like the image below.

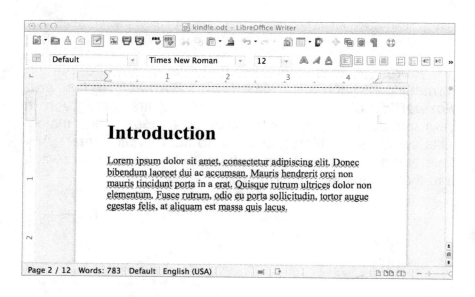

Inserting Photos

If your book will contain photos (even a cover image) there are a few things to know about them.

First, lets insert a photo into your document. To do that press enter to get to a new paragraph and then select *Insert*, *Picture*, *From File* in the menu.

Browse for the picture file that you want to insert, click on it, and then click the *Open* button.

One thing to keep in mind is that some Kindle devices have limited support for images. Some models are black and white while others are color. Older versions of Kindle software only support left aligned images. Because of these limitations, I prefer that my images always show up at 100% of the page width.

Highlight your image and then click on *Format*, *Picture* in the menu. On the *Type* tab check the *Relative* box under *Width* and then set the width to 100%. Leave *Height* as-is and check the *Keep ratio* box if it's not already checked. Click the *OK* button to save those changes.

Read that last paragraph again and look at the screen shot below. If you have multiple pictures in your book, you'll do this over and over again for each and every one of them.

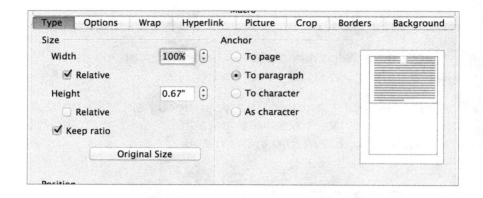

Depending on the original size of the image, you may not see this change in your document. Rest assured, though, that you did something important there.

You can also add a border to your image. To do that, click on the picture, to select it, and then select **Format**, **Picture** from the menu. This time click on the **Borders** tab. Click the full border icon (the arrow below) and then click the **OK** button.

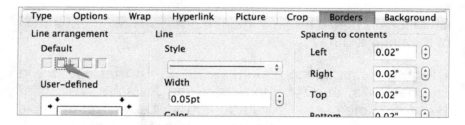

Your image should now display full width with a solid black border.

You can also paste images into your book. Amazon actually recommends against this, so I'll just gloss over it. To copy and paste and image, just copy your image to the clipboard from your favorite image editor and then paste it into a new paragraph. This works for me, but I haven't figured out why Amazon suggests against it, so I'll trust their advice and suggest you avoid copy and paste.

Making the TOC

We'll need a table of contents for our book. To create one, select *Insert*, *Indexes and Tables*, and then *Indexes and Tables* again from the menu.

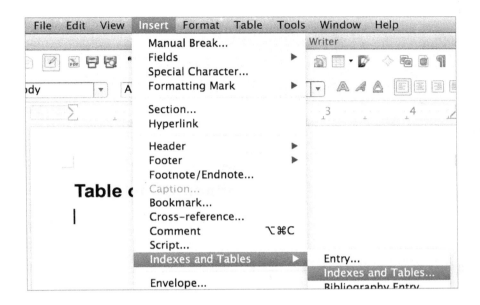

Because the kindle doesn't use page numbers, you'll also want to remove page numbers from your TOC. To do that, select the *Entries* tab then click on the button labeled **#** and then click on the *Chapter no.* button. The arrows in the image below should help you find all those things.

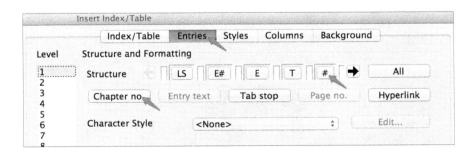

Your Table of Contents doesn't update automatically so it will start to get out of sync as you make changes to your document. To get things back in order, you'll need to update the Table of Contents periodically. The easiest way to do that is to select *Tools*, *Update*, *All Indexes and Tables* in the menu.

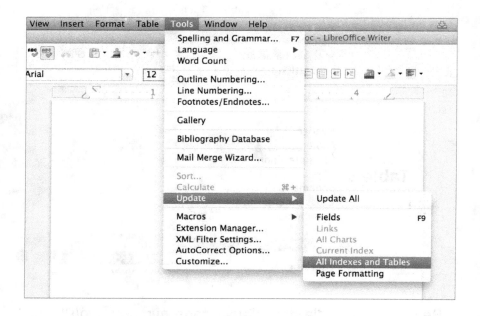

Adjusting Fonts

You can adjust the fonts for various sections of your book using the *Styles and Formatting* dialog that you used earlier. Open that using the **Format**, **Styles and Formatting** menu. In the dialog that opens, right click on the **Default** formatting item and then select **modify**.

In the next dialog that opens you'll be able to set the font and point size for the default text on the page. For this book I selected **Arial** as the font and **12pt** as the *Size*. Click **OK** to save your changes.

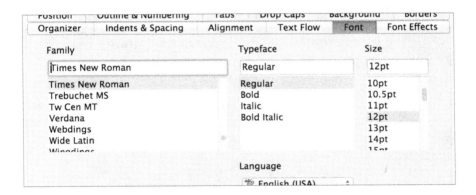

Note that this changes only the font in text that is marked as *Default* on the page. You've used *Default* text and *Heading 1* text in your book so far. Use the same process to modify the *Heading 1* font and size for the headings in your book.

If Everything Goes Wrong

If your document is all wrong at this point, you probably want to slow down and try again from the top. It may make more sense as you work through it a second time.

If you'd rather not, and you just want to get started writing your book, I'll bail you out here. I've created a document that you can use as a starting point. In this document I've already done all of this formatting for you. Hopefully you can download the doc file, open it in LibreOffice, and start writing. It will help a lot if you understand the formatting concepts though, so I still encourage you to try the setup from scratch on your own.

You'll find the template at the URL below. To use it, download it, save it locally, then open it and start editing.

http://joeldare.com/files/kindle_template.doc

That's it for book editing and we're almost done. Let's take a look at creating a cover and then publishing.

Creating Cover Art

You'll probably want to create a cover page for your book. The cover will be displayed on Amazon when your book is listed for sale.

Although I don't want to give you a full tutorial on creating a drawing in this book (whole books are written on the subject) LibreOffice does come with a nice tool for creating your cover art. Select **File**, **New**, **Drawing** from the menu to open up *LibreOffice Draw*.

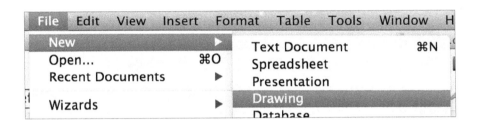

Now, set the drawing page to the same dimensions as your book. Again, we'll use 5.5" wide by 8.5" tall for the page size. Select **Format**, **Page** in the menu and then enter your **Width** and **Height** in the dialog that opens. Click the **OK** button to confirm that change.

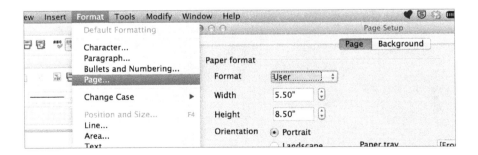

If you're outside the United States, use the same size you used on your first document.

Experiment with *LibreOffice Draw* a bit. You can add text, shapes, colors, and images to your cover art.

When your drawing is finished select **File**, **Export** from the menu. Select **PNG** in the **File type** drop down and save your cover art somewhere that you'll be able to find it easily later on.

Signup for Amazon KDP

Now that your book is started, it's time to create an Amazon Kindle Direct Publishing (KDP) account. You'll use KDP to upload your books to Amazon and to see your sales information.

Point your web browser to the KDP site at the URL below.

http://kdp.amazon.com

If you already have an Amazon account, you'll want to click the *Sign In* button on that page. If you don't, then click the *Sign Up* button. In either case, follow the Amazon prompts to create your account and then sign in to KDP.

Direct Publishing, the fast and
r books for sale in the Kindle

can self-publish your books on the Amazon
s self-published through KDP can participate
le for purchase on Kindle devices and Kindle
ac, BlackBerry, and Android-based devices.
hany languages - including English, German,
- and specify pricing in US Dollars, Pounds
information on our active community forum.

Sign in with your Amazon account

Sign in ▶

You will be signed in using our secure server

Don't have an Amazon account

Sign up ▶

English | **Deutsch** | **Français** | **Español** |
Italiano

Uploading to KDP

Once you have an account and are signed into KDP, it's time to list your book. Your book isn't finished yet, but you're probably eager to see what it looks like. You can upload a draft right now and publish it later on when it's complete and everything looks right to you.

Click the **Add new title** button to create your draft.

Now, in section 1, enter as many of your books details as you can. Fill out at least the **Book name**, **Description**, **Contributors**, and **Language** fields; they are all required.

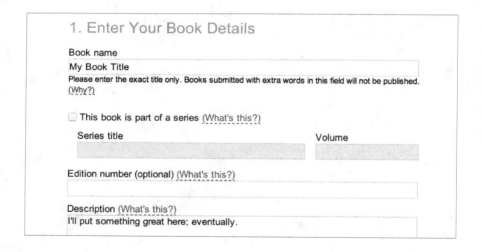

In section 2, verify your publishing rights. Click the radio button indicating either that you're publishing a Public Domain book or that you hold the necessary publishing rights. If this is your own book, written in your own words, and you don't have any legal agreements with anyone else, then you're the author and publisher and you hold the necessary publishing rights.

---

2. Verify Your Publishing Rights

Publishing rights status: (What's this?)

○ This is a public domain work.

○ This is not a public domain work and I hold the necessary publishing rights.

In section 3, select two categories that your book fits into. You're limited to two and I suggest you use both of them. Also, enter 7 keywords. Take your time, these are important for marketing. Choose words and categories that users are likely to use to find your book. Choosing keywords is a special art in its own right. Eventually you may want to experiment with them to see what keywords give you the most sales.

---

3. Target Your Book to Customers

Categories (What's this?)

    Add Categories

Search keywords (up to 7, optional): (What's this?)

                                                              7 keywords left

---

Next, upload your cover art. This is actually optional, but it can help your sales significantly. If you have cover art then click the **Browse for Image** button and select your cover art image.

In step 5, select one of the digital rights management options. Read Amazon's information about DRM by clicking on the **What's this?** Link. Personally, I do not enable DRM because I don't want to be restricted as a consumer so I give my readers the same courtesy. The choice is somewhat controversial though, so read their help and decide for yourself.

Finally, it's time to upload your book. Early on, we saved your book as a Microsoft Word 97 document. Click the **Browse for book** button, find that file you saved, highlight it, and click the **Open** button. Now click the **Upload book** button to start the upload and conversion process.

5. Upload Your Book File

Select a digital rights management (DRM) option: (What's this?)

○ Enable digital rights management

◉ Do not enable digital rights management

Book content file:

[   ]   [Browse for book...]

> Learn KDP content guidelines   [Upload book]
> Help with formatting

The website will spin for a while showing that your book is uploading. After that, it will show that the book is being converted to Kindle format. Although you can continue, we want to wait for the process to complete. When it's done you'll have options to preview the book as it will look on Kindle devices. Do that and look through your book to see how it looks on various devices. If you don't like something, make a change in LibreOffice and upload it again. You'll probably do this process dozens of times. You should do it often as you work on your book so that you don't get a bunch of surprises when your book is nearly complete.

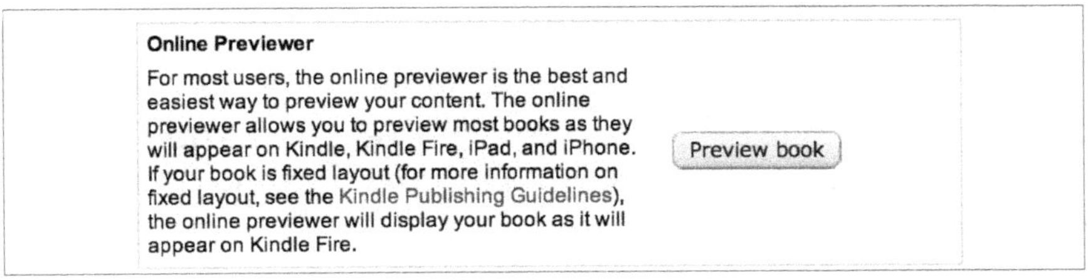

Online Previewer

For most users, the online previewer is the best and easiest way to preview your content. The online previewer allows you to preview most books as they will appear on Kindle, Kindle Fire, iPad, and iPhone. If your book is fixed layout (for more information on fixed layout, see the Kindle Publishing Guidelines), the online previewer will display your book as it will appear on Kindle Fire.

[Preview book]

Once everything in the preview checks out, your book is ready for publishing. Click the *Save and Continue* button to go on to set your pricing and publish your book. Publishing takes about 48 hours and you'll start to get paid for sales in 60 days.

Contact the Author

As you can tell, I'm not a professional author. I wrote this book because I wanted to help people get started writing their own Kindle book quickly and make a few dollars in the process.

I love reading comments, suggestions, and even criticism. If you have any feedback about the book, please send me email at the address below.

__joel@joeldare.com__